gone to the
dogs

Books by Robert F. Jones

FICTION:

Blood Sport, 1974

The Diamond Bogo, 1977

Slade's Glacier, 1981

Blood Root, (as Thomas Mordane), 1982

Blood Tide, 1990

Tie My Bones to Her Back, 1996

Deadville, 1998

The Run to Gitche Gumee, 2001

NONFICTION:

The Fishing Doctor: The Essential Tackle Box Companion, 1992

Upland Passage: A Field Dog's Education, 1992

Jake: A Labrador Puppy at Work and Play, 1992 (children's book)

African Twilight: The Story of a Hunter, 1995

Dancers in the Sunset Sky: The Musings of a Bird Hunter, 1996

On Killing: Meditations on the Chase, ed, 2001

The Hunter in My Heart: A Sportsman's Salmagundi, 2002

gone to the
dogs

life with my canine
companions

Robert F. Jones
with Louise Jones

Foreword by Dan Gerber
Photographs by Benno Jones

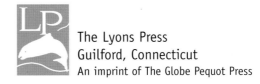

The Lyons Press
Guilford, Connecticut
An imprint of The Globe Pequot Press

The Lyons Press is an imprint of The Globe Pequot Press.

10   9   8   7   6   5   4   3   2   1

Printed in China

Designed by LeAnna Weller Smith

ISBN: 1-59228-220-2

Library of Congress Cataloging-in-Publication Data is available on file.

For Bob

FOREWORD

I'm sitting here with our yellow Labrador, Eudora, whom Debbie and I call Eudie, wondering how to begin my introduction to Bob and Louise Jones's moving, delightful, and instructive new book called *Gone to the Dogs*. I've known Bob and Louise since the early seventies, the era of their Simba and my Lily, for we noted our years by the dogs who were our companions, teachers, sounding boards, and alter egos.

I had just written my first piece for *Sports Illustrated,* and the magazine was sending Bob and me to Kenya to do a story on "The Last Great Safari" when I first visited the Jones's household in Somers, New York, prior to our departure for Nairobi. Simba was just entering late middle age, about eight years old as I recall; Lily, whom I had reluctantly left in Michigan, was a six-month-old pup; and Benno, who took the marvelous photographs that grace these pages, was thirteen and had just been awarded his brown belt in karate.

Bob and I shared many enthusiasms: auto racing—Bob covered racing for *Sports Illustrated,* and I had been a professional driver; Africa—we did two major safaris together under the cover of journalism; fly fishing; our love of and devotion to literature and good writing; and, of course, our preternatural attachment to our dogs.

Whenever Bob's magazine assignments brought him to the Midwest, he would schedule a stopover at our farm in western Michigan. I had given up bird hunting by that time, and Lily had never really been trained for hunting, but in honor of Bob's visit I would dig out my old Winchester 21 and accompany Bob and Lily through the swales and the poplar and sumac thickets along the edges of the beech, oak, and hemlock forest surrounding our house. These armed walks were autumnal idylls, not serious hunts, though on several occasions we brought home a grouse or two for the pot, and when Bob's visits occurred in the spring, the three of us would scour those same thickets for morel mushrooms with far greater success. But whether we used grouse or mushrooms as

our excuse, our real objective was simply to spend time together in the calming company of our canine companion and to say, sometimes, some of the best things we ever said.

Even though we may treat them as such, our dogs are not human. They are blessedly incapable of conceptual thinking or complex emotions, though if we are attentive to the ways in which they address us, we know them to be the pluperfect example of how we should be, a reflection of our most unencumbered selves. And if they are sad about their lowly status or the shortness of their lives, they leave it to us to be their regret. They are so placid and self-contained, Walt Whitman assures us, that "Not one is dissatisfied—not one is demented with the mania of owning things . . . Not one is respectable or unhappy over the whole earth."

In *The Diamond Bogo,* his roman à clef inspired by our travels together in Africa, Jones portrays himself as Bucky Blackrod, the hard-bitten, no-nonsense New York journalist, set against my character, Don McGavern, the poet/adventurer with the "plumey" voice. He describes Don's ebullient Norwegian elkhounds as "hirsute basketballs of caninity," a description which is neither hard-bitten nor no-nonsense. The truth is that for all his Hemingwayesque bravado and Marquezian imagination, Jones was, when it came to his dogs, one big baby, which, to anyone who has read *Jake* or *Upland Passage*, and lingered over William Eppridge's heart-melting photographs, will come as no surprise.

On a gray October morning in 1989, Bob and I drove an hour and a half from my home in Michigan to Grace and Myron Morris's Toynton Labradors Kennel to pick up our seven-week-old yellow pups, Jake and Willa. At first I assumed the tears edging down either side of Bob's nose were in response to the sharp autumn wind off Lake Michigan but then immediately realized the wind was neither that sharp nor strong. Bob's old hunting companion, Luke, was thirteen years old, facing what would likely be his last season in the field, and Bob had been living with the sadness we all carry through what we know must be our last weeks and months with someone we love, even though Jake's squirming puppy grunts soon had Bob laughing through his tears. As dog lovers we all know that the disparity between human and canine longevity, which can seem a cruel cosmic joke, is also a vital form of practice in the inevitable letting go of our own lives and of all those we hold dear. Our dogs, spared this fore-knowledge of loss, are constantly rousing us to the present, telling us with their plaintive looks and heavy breathing, "Put on your boots and let's get going. We'll never have this day again."

Twelve years later Jones called when we finally had to put Willa down. It rained all that dark winter day. Debbie and I built a fire and lay on the floor with Willa all morning and most of the afternoon while I read to her from *Leaves of Grass*. Not that she understood the words, but she lay, drowsy and content with the sound of my voice until our vet came in the evening. I held her on my lap, and she snoozed while he gave her the shot that extended her sleep indef-initely. A few pale drops of blood fell from her nose with her last breaths, and we left their stain on the carpet because we couldn't bear to scrub away this last trace of her. Eleven months later I called Bob to tell him how sorry I was that he'd lost Jake, and a scant month after that Louise called to tell us of Bob's passing.

Love for the new is love for the old. I don't know if that's an aphorism I coined or one I picked up somewhere along the way, but I embrace it. We can't replace any of the dogs of our lives, and we certainly can't replace our human loved ones, but when I hung up the phone after saying all the things we say to try to soothe what can't, at such a time, be soothed, my first thought was how glad I was that Bob had gotten a new pup to understudy Jake in his last season. It made it easier for me, at least, knowing Louise had Bart with her there in Vermont on that sad winter's night. And I know that, simply by his presence, Bart helped Louise find the courage and inspiration to complete this wonderful book.

Dan Gerber
Spring 2004

xiv

gone to the
dogs

BOB:

A NEW DOG IS ALWAYS AN ADVENTURE. With a puppy just weaned from the care of its mother (and the rowdy companionship of its littermates), the adventure is one of bonding: Will the newcomer accept you as the most important factor in its life? Will it adapt to its new home and the other members of its new family, human, canine, and perhaps even feline? How responsive will the puppy be to its new master's wishes and commands? Will its desire to please be strong enough to outweigh its desire to raise all kinds of puppy hell?

Among the things I love best in Labrador retrievers is the breed's consistency. One Lab is so very much like another in temperament and physique, companion-ability, and eagerness to be trained—in short, in its very character—that you could almost call them "cookie-cutter dogs." Yet within this consistency there's still plenty of room for individuality. Each Lab, no matter how closely it adheres to the breed's paradigm, has a distinct though subtle personality of its own. Only when you've lived with a dog for a while, watching it grow from puppyhood to maturity, do these traits become evident.

Peter was the first of my six Labradors. When we got him in 1965, my wife, Louise, and I had two small children: our son, Benno, who was then three-and-a-half years old, and our daughter, Leslie, age six. Though neither of us had ever owned a Lab, we knew that in addition to being fine, all-purpose gundogs, Labs made excellent house-hold pets and were just plain terrific with kids. Rambunctious children could climb all over a Labrador, pound on him like a black-pelted drum, pull his ears, even ride him like a pony without provoking so much as a growl. We got Peter as an eight-week-old pup from a litter belonging to friends of Louise's family. Even at that tender age he was laid-back, easygoing, always had a look of mild wonderment on his face, and a wide, happy, Opie Taylor grin, anticipating what we would be up to next.

It was with Peter that I first saw a gundog discover the meaning of life. He took readily to retrieving: at first sticks, then a rubber ball, finally a canvas-covered retrieving dummy. But though he followed me afield after grouse and woodcock and saw a number of them killed, he couldn't seem to connect the dots between the retrieving dummy and the dead bird. I hoped in time it would come, and later that fall it did. It happened during one memorable hunt through the nine hundred acres of fields and second-growth hardwoods that rose behind our home in the town of Somers, the northernmost township in Westchester County, New York. Late one autumn afternoon we were pounding an overgrown field on the back side of a ridge hunting uphill, with me on the right side of a stone wall and Peter paralleling me on the wall's far side. Peter pushed through some pucker-brush toward the wall and accidentally flushed a ruffed grouse. It exploded under his nose, a loud russet-gray firebomb of flurried speed, and lined out quartering away from me. An easy shot, and Peter heard the gun go *pow*, saw the grouse jolt to the shot pattern and fall heavily, tip over tail, into a clump of young hardhack at the top of the field. I was watching him as the bird thumped down and a cloud of feathers fell gently from the sky. On the instant, Peter's brown eyes caught fire, bright with a sudden epiphany—So this is what it's all about! Without a moment's hesitation he dashed into the thicket to make a perfect retrieve.

That was the turning point. From then on Peter was always eager to hunt, tireless in the field, with a keen nose for grouse or woodcock scent, a bull-like strength in the densest of cover, and a tender mouth on the retrieve. I could look forward (I thought) to at least ten years of excellent upland hunting with Peter, but it was not to be. The following spring he disappeared. I had let him out unaccompanied for his morning "spritz," during which he customarily made a circuit of the house, marking his territory, and sometimes trotted down to the brook that ran through our property for a quick drink, but I'd never known him to cross the wooden bridge that spanned the trout stream unless I was with him. Across the bridge a trail led up into the vast acreage we hunted, and he always waited for me before heading into that endless covert. When he failed to return to the back door that morning, I went out and whistled for him, shouted his name again and again. Fearing the worst, I walked the road that fronted our property, afraid that he might have been hit by a passing car. Then I hiked our favorite bird covers, calling for him, firing occasional shots in hopes that he would come galloping back to take part in the action. He was nowhere to be found. A team of dognappers had been working the area, we later learned, trolling the byroads of upper Westchester with a bitch in heat. Peter would have licked his chops and come grinning from ear to ear. When dogs of whatever breed caught the scent and came sniffing around for the source, it was an easy matter to capture and sell them to medical laboratories. I vowed then that if I ever caught a dognapper, he would pay the ultimate price.

Heartbroken at Peter's loss and my own stupidity, but mostly at the promise unfulfilled by his early disappearance, I shied away from getting another Labrador and

instead acquired a German short-haired pointer pup whom we named Max. He proved to be an excellent bird dog—an instinctive pointer, hard-charging but very light-footed when he scented and approached game birds. Yet Max, for all his skills in the field, lacked the warm personality, the infectious charm of a Lab. He was a one-man dog who lived for hunting. To Max, our kids were just a couple of very inferior,

6

very clumsy, two-legged gundogs who couldn't scent the difference between a woodcock and a tweety-bird. Clearly we needed another Labrador.

Simba, a yellow Lab, was eighteen months old when he joined our household. As far as I know he'd never hunted before we got him—his previous owners were a sedentary English couple living in Scarsdale who had to move back to Britain for business reasons. Britain had very strict quarantine laws, and they felt it would be too cruel for Simba to be locked up for six months in a government kennel to ensure that he didn't have rabies.

A strong, confident dog who weighed 105 pounds in fighting trim, Simba confronted the world with a cocky, wiseass, Bruce Willis–like grin. He took to the field as if he'd been hunting from puppyhood. He was already a splendid retriever when we got him, having learned on sticks, balls, Frisbees, and the like, so game birds came easy. In twelve years of hunting, he never failed to find a bird that I'd dropped. Yet he had one incurable vice: he always insisted on devouring the first bird I killed each year—crunching them down in about three fast bites, bones, feathers, beaks, claws and all—though oddly enough he never ruffled a feather on the birds that followed.

He was also a fine retriever of fish. A quarter mile down the road from where we lived was the Croton Reservoir, a tepid, island-dotted bouillabaisse of black bass, bullfrogs, sunfish, crappies, and perch both yellow and white. Often I took the dogs with me when I visited the reservoir for a morning or evening of fly fishing. Max paid no attention to the fish I hooked, preferring to scour the adjacent woods for feathered prey. Simba, being a natural-born water dog, took fishing as seriously as he did waterfowl hunting. He would sit near my feet as I cast, watch the drop of the fly, the rise, the hookup, and then launch himself into the water as if from a duck blind. A few powerful strokes and he was out to the fish; he would surface dive and somehow manage to grab the hapless perch or sunfish without getting stuck by its spear-tipped dorsal fin, and bring it back to me proudly, head high, without harming a single scale. The fish always survived this ordeal, and I was able to release them in good health if I cared to.

One afternoon, Louise accompanied me to the reservoir and diverted Simba, while I fished on the other side of a copse of trees, by throwing sticks out into the water for him to retrieve. After a while her arm tired, so she had him sit. He did so for a few minutes, but then suddenly leapt back into the water and swam far offshore. I thought he might have spotted a duck or perhaps a gull out there, but no, he grabbed something heavy and began dragging it back to dry land. It proved to be a waterlogged tree trunk, about twenty feet long, that must have weighed more than a hundred pounds. When he'd dragged it up on the strand, he sat dutifully, wagging his tail and gazing eagerly up at my wife, expecting her to sling it back out there for another retrieve . . .

I hunted Simba in tandem with Max for upland birds, and they made a splendid team. At the merest whiff of a grouse or woodcock, Max would zero in on it and lock up on point. Then Simba would circle out beyond the bird and move back in, pinning it in place to deny it running room. He had an uncanny ability to anticipate a grouse's logical escape route. Once I was in position and on my command, Simba would step in and pounce to get the bird airborne. He was perfect on the retrieve. Oh, there were occasional lapses of decorum, but that's to be expected in dogs with a strong sense of self. On warm days in the early autumn, for instance, Simba would sometimes call a time out in the business proceedings and break away from the line we were hunting to seek out an old cellar hole that was filled with cool water from a spring seep. The stone cellar was maybe six feet deep, with rainwater filling it to the halfway mark. Simba would plunge in with a mighty splash and paddle a few quick laps, deaf to my plaintive pleas—"Come, Simba! Please, pleeeeeease come out of there! COME HERE, you blankety-blank mutt!" Finally I'd lean the shotgun against a nearby tree, get down on my knees, and snag Simba's collar as he swam by, then haul him dripping, squirming, and mucky from the swimming hole, where, of course, he'd shake himself dry as he stood beside me.

Over the years, he made hundreds of fine saves for me on doubtful birds, but the one that sticks most fondly in my memory is The Case of the Trickster in the Treetop. It was a bleak, cold day, the sky hard and gray as pig iron, with ankle-deep

snow swirling across the ground, and Max had pointed a cock pheasant in a dense stand of sumac flanking an old stone wall. The rooster flushed wild as I worked my way into position, and though I threw a forlorn shot at it, I missed. We watched it sail downhill and land in the bare, topmost branches of a tall ash tree at the edge of the woods. Down we went after him, but the cock wouldn't fly from his lofty perch until I threw a snowball at him. Then I grabbed up the gun and fired again, and again I missed. Of course, the bird flew back uphill. A keen, stiff, northwest wind scoured the stubble as we stumped back up the way we'd come. I'd marked the pheasant down along a fence line dividing a mowed field. The bird was nowhere to be seen. He couldn't have run off; we'd have spotted him. I set the dogs to sniffing the entire length of the fence line. Sure-nosed Max charged on, headlong and headstrong as always on a hot scent, but it was Simba who finally found the bird hiding beneath a fallen strand of barbed wire around which a foot-long tuft of grass no higher than my ankles had grown. The big Lab glanced back at me, smirked, then flushed the trickster.

When he brought the dead rooster back to my hand, I finally felt vindicated in my choice of gundog. It was Peter's promise fulfilled.

10

THEN MAX BEGAN TO COUGH, lose weight, and refuse to eat; he moped around the house. Our vet couldn't diagnose his symptoms, although he agreed that something was wrong; Max was only three years old. We visited another vet, and then a third, Bob Schimmelman. "There's a new disease," he told us. "It's called heartworm, and it used to be found in dogs in the South, but it seems to have traveled north." We learned that heartworm is indeed a worm, transmitted to the dog by a mosquito bite. The adult worms can live in the dog for as long as five years. Now most veterinarians test dogs annually for evidence of heartworm, and those that test positive can be treated successfully. Those that test negative can take preventive medicine once a month in a tasty chewable form. Several tests proved that Dr. Schimmelman's hunch was right, but it was too late for Max. Medication and meals of raw liver didn't help. One morning two weeks after the diagnosis, Bob woke early to the sound of Simba moaning. He ran down to the kitchen and found Max dead on the floor, Simba backed up in a corner, staring at his hunting buddy. Max was one of the first victims of heartworm in Westchester County. We never knew how he got it or how long he'd had it. Fortunately, Simba tested negative. For all his faults as a family dog, Max was a brilliant hunter and Bob mourned his death.

Once more, we were a one dog family.

As the years passed we talked from time to time about getting another dog. When Simba was nine years old, Benno and I decided to surprise Bob with a puppy for his birthday, which was May 26. We figured that the spring was the perfect time for training a new puppy. Our first, Peter, was born in late January and came to us in early March. I still remember rising before light, shivering into my robe and throwing on a coat, shoving my feet into boots, and hurrying Peter into the snowy backyard for his morning ablutions. Housebreaking a dog in the summer seemed far preferable. I began looking at ads and asked our veterinarian how to find a good litter. Since then I've learned, and firmly believe, that people should select their own dogs. Giving a dog as a gift can create countless problems: Does the person really want a dog at that time? Is it the right kind of dog? Who will train and care for the dog? Although I knew the answers to most of these questions, we still should have allowed Bob to make the choice. But we didn't.

We also didn't follow most of the rules for finding a proper puppy. Books on dog selection advise not purchasing from a "backyard breeder" but from a reputable professional breeder; you're also told to get references, investigate the breeder's reputation, and certainly to view the litter in advance of making a selection. Choose the individual puppy by temperament and conformity to breed type— don't choose the boldest or shyest, the books tell us. But choosing a puppy is usually an emotional issue, unless you are very serious about your plans for an adult dog. If you want an excellent hunting dog or a dog bred for protection or for herding, you'll be very careful about making the choice. We knew Bob would want a hunting dog, so we zeroed in on that.

I found a litter in Rockland County, across the Hudson from our home in Westchester, and talked with the breeder. She didn't own a kennel—the dam was her family pet, from show stock, but the sire was a hunting dog from Maine, bred for the field. There were nine puppies in the litter, five of them black, two of the males were available, and they were seven weeks old, the perfect age for separation from the litter. While Bob was in Indianapolis covering the Memorial Day race for *Sports Illustrated,* Benno and I drove across the Tappan Zee Bridge on a bright, windy day. Despite our research on selection, all was forgotten as soon as we saw the litter—nine plump bodies squirming on the lawn. A black pup noticed us and ran to Benno, wagging its tiny tail. Benno reached down, scooped it up, and the puppy immediately licked him. That was it. We were smitten. Fortunately, it was a male and available for sale. He curled up on Benno's lap on the drive home, while we talked excitedly about how to introduce him to Simba and how to present him to Bob. So much for research.

The next day, Bob returned from Indianapolis. We stashed the puppy in Leslie's room and Benno and I nonchalantly welcomed Bob home with a birthday card. "Well thanks," he said, a little puzzled. Birthdays are important events in our family, and we never give just a card. Then Leslie walked into the room with the puppy in her arms. Bob was delighted and named him Buck. Training began.

All puppies chew, each with a preference. Peter liked shoes and boots, Max nibbled on chair legs. Buck was a natural born confetti-maker. He'd quickly rip any magazine or newspaper within his reach into thin strips, then he'd roll on them. If we were going out of the house for a while and closed him in the bathroom (this was before we discovered the sense and ease of crate training), he would unroll and shred the toilet paper. Simba tolerated him, but wasn't too keen about cuddling, so Buck would often crawl under a skirted armchair or its hassock for a snooze. It was only when I moved the furniture to vacuum under it that I discovered he had pulled off the covering underneath the seat and had excavated into the chair and hassock cushions, shredding the filling as he did paper. There was no keeping him away from these two pieces of furniture, and we gave up. They were in need of reupholstery anyway, and we just sent them off to be recovered once Buck grew too large to fit beneath them—a process of a few months.

Buck was large boned, but not as handsome as Simba or Peter. His snout was a little sharp—snipey Bob called it—but he had a typical Lab anvil-shaped head and a happy, often goofy, look in his eyes. Simba was willing to allow Buck to trot along with him outside, but we noticed he often played keep-away with the puppy. With Max gone, Simba was Number One, and he didn't want anyone to forget it. The next fall, when Buck was six months old, Bob and Simba began training the puppy for his job: flushing and retrieving game birds. Buck learned quickly, although

Simba was jealous of his retrieves, and Bob often had to hold the older dog back to let the puppy fetch a fallen bird. Training went well that first season, and Bob had high hopes for another dynamic duo. But there wasn't another season for Buck.

The next spring a friend visiting for the weekend woke very early and let the dogs out of the house on a Saturday morning. Simba came back within ten minutes for his breakfast; Buck had disappeared. An hour later Bob, Benno, and I were awake (Leslie was at college) and decided to wait a while. He might have been distracted by an animal in the woods. Our friend was apologetic. "After all," she said, "this is the country." She thought you could just let pets run. We patiently explained to her that there were too many temptations for loose dogs: deer to run after, females in heat, cars using our road as a shortcut to the interstate a few miles distant. After an hour I could wait no longer and jumped into the car, driving up and down the road calling for Buck. No sight of him. With trepidation I decided to try the highway and about a mile up noticed a black garbage bag on the side of the road. As I neared, I realized it was Buck, his body so crumpled and still that I'd thought it was a limp bag. I still dream about finding him and relive my horror at mistaking him for a bag of trash. I lifted him into the car and raced home, told Bob to call the veterinarian, and sped the ten minutes to the animal hospital.

I kept telling myself he might still be alive. Of course, he wasn't. He had been killed instantly, and either bounced or was shoved to the side of the road. The dogs must have run into the woods behind our house, then made their way down to the highway. Simba had road sense and ran back home through the woods. Naive Buck ran onto the road. Had Simba seen Buck killed? Had he run home to tell us? Or, we wondered, had the jealous Simba seen the accident and trotted home happy to be rid of the competition? We'll never know, of course, but it was a dreadful experience. We sat, stunned and weeping, most of the day. We assured our friend that she should not blame herself, which was true. We should have warned her the night before not to let the dogs out alone. But our relationship with her—a pal since college days—was never the same.

Buck had been a difficult dog to train, and we decided that we would do a better job the next time. We also revived a discussion of several years earlier, that we should move to a more remote area. We had stayed in Westchester because our children were happy there, with many friends and school activities; Bob could commute to Manhattan in a little more than an hour, and my family lived nearby. But the proximity of the highway and beyond it, the interstate, and increasing traffic zooming past our home as new houses were built north of us, convinced us that a change was near. Our daughter was already in college, and our son had only one more year of high school.

But before that came Luke.

The winter after Buck died, Bob's colleague at *Sports Illustrated,* Bob Boyle, told us his outstanding black Lab Guin had just had a large litter—all black puppies. Bob Boyle owned the sire of the litter, too, and both dogs had field lines and were excellent hunters. How could we resist taking a look? People like us rarely "take a look." If we don't want a puppy, we don't even look, because it's too hard to say no. The Boyles lived on the banks of the Hudson across from West Point, in a rambling old stone house with one room devoted to the pups. It was a roiling ant hill of ten black bodies, with an exhausted Guin happy to allow Bob, Benno, and me to pick them up. We said we'd really have to think about it, and we'd come back the next week. Bob Boyle said in his gravely voice, "These puppies are driving us all nuts. If you want one take it home with you now!" After hardly any discussion, Bob made the choice this time—a well-formed male.

Bob Boyle had one caveat: Guin's full name was Literary Guinevere, and he wanted all of the pups from the litter to be AKC registered with a name starting with Literary. "I hope that doesn't mean another paper shredder," I said. Bob liked a one-syllable, simple name for his dogs, so we had already decided on Luke. (Simba had been given that clumsy name by the English couple, although with his size and enormous head, he did resemble a lion.) Benno suggested, "How about Literary Lucifer? He's as black as the devil," and that was it.

Luke was smart, shy with Simba so he didn't antagonize the older dog, and trained quickly. He chewed a little on the furniture, but didn't cause much damage.

He lived for hunting and, as second choice, for retrieving his Frisbee. He would even sleep on his back with the Frisbee on his stomach, at his side, or dangling from an eyetooth. He could catch it on the fly, and would run like the wind to retrieve it. In fact, Bob said he was a retrieving fool.

Luke was a little more than a year old when we moved to Vermont. During our fifteen years in northern Westchester, our town had changed from exurbs (with even a few remaining farms) to commuter-land. With our daughter in college and our son about to go, we decided it was time to move far away from crowds. One week after Benno was graduated from high school we moved to southwestern Vermont, to a thirty-six-square-mile town with four villages and a population of 608. Our house is a white clapboard farmhouse built in 1826, with thirty-five acres and a brook, facing a dirt road. The yard around the house, with its rolling lawn and flower beds and two meadows—one across the road and one behind the house—make up about five acres. The rest is woods, filled with a few very old apple trees, but mainly birch, aspen, various types of maple, hickory, and the occasional oak. Across the road we face a mountain, which was planted with apple trees after World War I; many remain, their gnarled and twisted branches still producing tiny apples that I often pick in the autumn and turn into apple sauce and pie. The large meadow behind the house climbs up Bear Mountain, which tops out at twenty-three hundred feet. Except for one neighbor along the side of the meadow, our view is of waving meadow grass and wildflowers in the summer and deer-tracked snow in the winter, surrounded as far as you can see with trees. On hikes we discovered a number of old cellar holes from long-vanished cabins that dot the upper elevations along the tumbling brook. In addition to the deer, the land is home to wild turkeys that eat grasshoppers in the meadow in late summer, rabbits, snowshoe hares, martens, beavers, red and gray squirrels, chipmunks, raccoons, woodchucks, red and gray foxes, coyotes, bears, and the random moose, as well as all types of mice, moles and voles, and a multitude of birds: many songbirds; snowy, downy, and pileated woodpeckers; red-tailed, red-shouldered, and Harris hawks; goshawks; egrets; and Bob's favorite, grouse and woodcock.

Within a month of moving to Vermont, Simba died. His heart, liver, and kidneys just gave out, and the poor old guy put his head in my lap one evening and, over a half hour, his breathing became weaker and weaker, and finally stopped. He'd been a treasured member of the family.

Luke was smaller than any of our other Labs, but he was dead serious about hunting. The Frisbee was a natural replacement for game birds, which even Luke realized were not constantly falling from the sky. Although Luke was as loveable as all of his breed, he was not quite as warm and cuddly as Peter, Simba, and Buck, nor our later Labs Jake and Bart. He loved to sit in the car, and whenever a car door was open, he would jump in and sit in the driver's seat, staring out the windshield with a serious look on his face. However, he hated to be in a moving car and would stand up in the back seat, no matter how long the trip, barking or wailing, constantly shifting to keep upright. We figured that he associated the car with going hunting and was so excited that he couldn't control himself once the car began moving.

When Luke was about five years old, Bob was invited to New Brunswick for a fall bird hunt. "Bring your dog along," Bob was told. The hotel was strictly for bird hunters and allowed dogs in the rooms. Luke stood in the back of the car, moaning, for most of the ten-hour drive through Vermont, New Hampshire, Maine, and into Canada. When they arrived, he jumped out of the car and followed Bob into the hotel and up to the room, but while Bob was in the dining room at dinner, the sounds of Luke whining and barking reverberated throughout the hotel. As soon as they went outside, Luke stood by the car door. "Get me out of here," he seemed to say. "I want to go home." He finally quieted down and was as splendid in the field as always, but travel was not his thing, and Bob told me that he carried on most of the trip home.

As Luke grew older he developed arthritis, very common in Labs, but that never stopped him in the field. From Bob's gunning diary for 1987 when Luke was going on ten years old:

October 15: Hunted in the seep behind town on a hot Indian summer day. In the seep itself, Luke flushed a woodcock right to me. I turned and took it going away. It pitched into heavy briars but Luke sniffed him out (it was a male) and retrieved. A fine job by Luke.

October 27: This was as fine a day as I've had with Luke—or any other dog. It was Luke's best day ever—he really knows what it's all about—damn fine in his old age. On a hunch that late-season flight birds came down on last night's low-20s cold, went up the road side of the cover. Luke got birdy right away—watched him work a woodcock up just where I'd walked through downed oak leaves. One shot . . . Then two grouse (staggered) in the first swale. I got the first on the second barrel, then a woodcock on the second barrel; another came but no shot . . . Then two more woodcock out from under an oak downhill. We circled to the seep cover and Luke became very birdy on the edge of the seep. A bird went out downstream. I was hung up on a thorn apple, cleared, missed the first barrel, got it on the second . . . All Luke's retrieves were well worked out and fine.

October 30: Luke worked close and thoroughly all morning long. No complaints. He has become a fine flushing retriever. Luke nosed out a woodcock in the upper right corner of "Seep Square" but no shot. Then I flushed a woodcock by the leafy oak and killed it in one shot, and Luke retrieved it. Then I shot another easy one, and again Luke made a perfect retrieve. Later, Luke put up an easy woodcock in the aspens, a classic up-and-out rise, which I blew! All told, a good, fast morning hunt with Luke performing admirably, I less so.

Luke was not an aggressive dog and cringed a little when he met other dogs, especially barking males. He was friendly with people, but mainly if they'd throw his Frisbee. Benno called him a wimp. We joked that should a burglar break into the house, Luke would probably welcome the thief and then offer him the Frisbee. But no matter how well you think you know your dog, be prepared for surprises.

One of our frequent visitors when we first moved to Vermont was our plumber, Jack Stannard, a stocky Vermonter with a wry sense of humor and a passion for hunting and fishing. He became fond of Luke and was a sucker for the Frisbee. When Luke identified Jack's truck approaching the driveway, he would run to the kitchen door, greeting Jack with the Frisbee dangling from his mouth, tail wagging furiously. Jack always gave the Frisbee a few throws before getting to work.

One morning Jack called to say he had left a large wrench in the cellar the day before, and he needed it for the day's work at another house. Bob found the wrench and told Jack he'd leave it just inside the back door. We had to go to the bank in Manchester, but the door would be unlocked. When we returned home the wrench was gone and Luke was snoozing in the living room. That evening Jack called. "You have some guard dog there," he told Bob. "Guard dog?" Bob replied, "That wimp!" Jack told us that Luke charged him as he entered the empty house and backed him in a corner for more than fifteen minutes, barking, snarling, and carrying on like a Doberman. Jack finally got him to quiet down and sniff his hand. When Luke realized it was his Frisbee-throwing pal, he backed off. Jack got out of the house fast. The next time Jack came it was as though the incident had never happened. Luke was overjoyed to see him. With the house empty, he had assumed the duties of a watchdog.

As readers of Bob's books and magazine articles know, in the fall of 1989 Jake joined our household. Bob's great friend, the writer Dan Gerber, had recently lost his beloved yellow Lab, Lily, and traced her bloodlines to the outstanding Toynton Kennels in Zeeland, Michigan, run by Grace Morris and her husband, Myron. Dan called Bob with the good news during the summer, telling him that the Toynton dogs were superb and a litter was on the way. Did we want one? How could we resist? Luke was aging, and we liked the idea of alternating black and yellow Labs. Bob agreed to take one of the puppies. Jake and Dan's Willa were born on August 14, and seven weeks later Bob and our friend Sean Donovan drove to Michigan to pick up the puppy. Jake was a joy from the start—smart, cuddly, bold, obedient, with a hunter's instinct but eager to learn from Luke. He was the ideal Lab combination: a fine hunter and a wonderful companion, and a gentleman to boot.

Jake was going on two when Luke died, and for more than a year we debated what our menagerie would welcome next. When our children were growing up we had, in addition to the dogs, a constantly expanding and contracting assortment of cats (with litters every spring until we wised-up and had them spayed). In addition, our daughter, Leslie, kept pet gerbils; our son had a boa constrictor named Snoopy for two years as well as a passing parade of frogs and fish, and finally, when he was in high school, a cockatiel. By the time Jake joined us, we had two older cats in addition to a kitten, which joined us about two months before we got Jake. A woman who worked at the bookstore where I am a bookseller came in one morning with a box of kittens. Of course, I took one. He had fleas and the first thing Bob and I did was bathe him. He struck out at Bob, ripping a good slice in his wrist. "Ouch!" he groaned. "This cat's name is Spike."

Our choice of another dog was solved by Donna Judge, the wife of Bob's friend Joe Judge. She had a Jack Russell terrier named Mrs. B (the mate of the Judges's first Jack Russell, Boomer) and she was expecting. Many years earlier we had been charmed by Dudley, a feisty Russell owned by our friend the photographer Stephen Green-Armytage and his wife, Judy. What a strange addition to the household it would be, we agreed. Let's do it. So on a hot, late-August weekend,

21

Bob drove to the Judges's house in Maryland and returned with Rosalind Russell, age seven weeks, weight three pounds. I kept Jake in the house as Bob picked Rozzie out of the car. We were afraid he'd think she was dinner. But, as usual, Jake was a gentleman, inquisitively sniffing the tiny puppy, licking her stomach, and later just staring curiously at this little wonder.

Roz was a delight. Like all Jack Russells, she was fearless, constantly in motion when she wasn't sleeping, her bright eyes darting at the slightest movement, barking at dropping leaves and cars two miles down the road. She stood in the front seat of the car, looking out the window and yapping at any animal, from field mouse to cow, along the road. Within a week she had the laid-back Jake under her spell; the cats leapt on a high shelf when she came into a room. Russells are quick studies. She housebroke quickly and learned the commands to come, sit, stay, and heel. She bonded with Jake right away and followed him wherever he went. Bob and I would stand at the door and call them, then laugh until we gasped as they sped through the field to the house—Jake galloping with grace, Roz keeping up with him even though she took four strides to his one, her bowlegs churning so fast they looked like wheels.

Jack Russells were bred to tunnel down holes after foxes, and Roz certainly liked to "go to ground." She chased chipmunks into their holes, digging furiously, sometimes so deep that only her tail, wagging nonstop, would indicate where she was; the tail was a great handle to drag her out of the excavation. But amazingly, Roz took to hunting. Perhaps because she followed Jake everywhere, she made such a fuss when Bob and Jake got into the truck without her that Bob began taking her along. She learned quickly and became a great flushing dog, burrowing under sharp thorns where Jake couldn't fit. However, Jake was the retriever, and she learned from the beginning she must stand aside and allow him to pick up the fallen bird. She also loved the water, and when Bob took her fishing, she'd jump in after his cast and often grab the startled fish and swim it back to shore in her mouth.

BOB:

NOT EVERYONE WOULD AGREE, but Louise and I feel that dogs make great bed companions. During cold winter nights in Vermont, they are invaluable. It's not a good idea—but few of us are strong enough to resist a puppy's wheedling, its clear desire to sleep with us. Jake's an exception. Our bedroom is on the second floor of the house, and for some unexplained reason he doesn't like to climb stairs, so spends the nights snugged down on his Orvis dog pad near the kitchen woodstove.

Each dog seemed to prefer a different sleeping position: Roz liked to lie sideways between us, so she could do her nocturnal isometric exercises, front paws on my butt, back paws in Louise's lower back, then sideways push-ups until at one time or another she had pushed one or both of us out of bed. Simba, despite his size, was no problem: he curled up at the foot of the bed and rarely moved throughout the night. Luke, too, was a considerate bedmate, curling up into a tight, black, foot-warming ball between our feet. If Louise or I shifted position during the night, he would sigh resignedly and move over whenever we nudged him.

In defiance of the laws of physics, dogs seem able to increase their weight at will. A dog like Roz, who weighed about fifteen pounds, could feel as if she weighed fifty when you tried to lift or budge her. Most of our dogs were early risers, except for slug-a-bed Roz, who could sleep under the covers until nine in the morning if she felt like it. Often we would be in the kitchen having a second cup of tea, breakfast long over, when she would finally hop down the stairs, her sleepy eyes poking through the banister.

Then, all of a sudden, Jake was twelve years old. And all of a sudden, I was sixty-seven. It happened too fast. That's another dirty trick life plays on us: it speeds up the passage of time just when we're running out of that precious commodity. It's hard to believe that Jake is an old dog now, and I an old man. Only yesterday we were in our prime. Deep down I had hoped, selfishly I suppose, that I might die before Jake passed on, that he might be my last dog and I'd never have to go through the heartbreak of loss again.

Still, whatever lay in store for us, I had to admit that the intervening years, fast as they'd sped by, had been full of great moments.

Autumn 1995. Jake at the height of his powers: We enter the swamp before dawn, wobbling our way over ice-slicked duckboards to the duck blind. Trees and snags and clumps of dead weed loom spectral in the dark. I tell Jake to sit. The cold water nearly submerges his thick, otterine tail, but he doesn't seem to mind. I rest my own butt on a "shooting stick" hammered into the half-frozen muck. Some shooting stick. It's a two-by-four topped with a six-inch-wide crosspiece. Very narrow, very hard.

A thin screen of boards and brush shields us from the water. Low clouds spit occasional flurries of sleet and corn snow. "Fine weather for ducks," I tell Jake. He grins up at me and his tail slaps the water. We can hear them talking out there in the flooded timber, the happy inconsequential chatter of their tribe, wondering what the day will hold. The chuckle of teal, the breathy whistle of wood ducks. I toss out the decoys. They fall in a lifelike spread.

It's just light enough to read my watch when a clot of indistinct shapes whizzes in from our left to splash down in front of the blind. Jake shivers, whiffing them. Duck scent, hot and oily and delicious. He looks up into my eyes, begging me to stand and shoot. "Too early, boy," I whisper. "Five minutes more till they're legal."

From far across the swamp, perhaps half a mile away, comes a sudden flurry of gunfire. Someone is breaking the law. Again Jake looks at me, quizzical. The ducks

are out there. Why don't you shoot? I shake my head. "It wouldn't do for us to get arrested, boy. Game wardens have sharp ears, and accurate watches, too."

We wait out the final minutes, counting down the last few agonizing seconds . . . Three, two, one . . .

"Okay, we're legal."

I stand. Ducks explode from the water in every direction. Foot-long flames from my gun barrels light the blind—ducks freeze-framed for an instant in the flash, then falling, hitting the water with silver splashes. When we look up a moment later, the light to the east has turned red.

There's no sound of thrashing on the water out there. Neither of the ducks I'd hit are moving. Jake waits for the signal to fetch them. His body is shaking with repressed action.

"Let's wait a bit longer, boy," I tell him. "This is the hot time, the first few minutes of daylight. You can pick up those birds later. They're not going anywhere."

Over the next twenty minutes it's nonstop action. Ducks come and go like air traffic over O'Hare. I drop some, miss others. I swing fast on a wood duck lining out left-to-right through the tops of the drowned trees, just within range of my twelve-gauge Beretta. Bang! Then bang again . . . the drake staggers to the second shot, slanting down far into the stumps and snags. It will be a long retrieve.

In seven years of waterfowl hunting I had never worked Jake in flooded timber. But now it's time to send him out for his first retrieve in the most difficult situation a Labrador can face. Frankly, though he's never disappointed me, either in the uplands or on waterfowl, I'm a bit worried. The water over which these ducks have fallen is studded with stumps, snags, blowdowns, and puckerbrush, all interspersed with clusters of dense, yellow-brown spartina grass that masks the water beyond. The bottom is thick, black muck. Jake will have to swim and wade both, while still maintaining the line I give him for a retrieve. I lead him to the exit gap at the front of the blind and point out a wood duck floating belly up not twenty yards off. "Fetch dead, Jake!"

All the while I was shooting, I'd been aware of Jake's eyes on me, marking the direction of my gun barrels each time I pulled the trigger. No doubt he could tell from the expression in my eyes if I hit or miss. What's more, all dogs have an inner ear that can shut down to filter out extraneous background noises, so Jake may well have concentrated only on the splashes of ducks hitting the water, and from those sounds gotten a rough idea of their range and direction. Whatever the case, he knew just where each of the downed birds was floating and retrieved them in apple-pie order when I told him to.

He hit the water in a flat racing dive. I saw him lift his nose as he neared the wood duck, saw his eyes flit over through the next screen of spartina. Then I made out the form of another dead duck out there, just behind the grass. He'd smelled it, spotted it, and marked it for his next retrieve. Now he brought the first bird in and handed it off to me. He looked back to the second bird, then up at me. I gave him the direction line with my hand. "Fetch!"

No problem . . .

Next up was a green-winged teal that had slanted down dead, out of sight, perhaps a hundred yards deep into the swamp. I sent Jake out in that general direction, but he went only halfway before getting turned around in a vain attempt to bull through a tangle of snags. He swam back toward the blind. I stepped down into the water and waded over to him, turned him around, and gave him a fresh line on the teal. This time Jake wisely swam around the snags. I lost sight of him for a few moments, then heard him splashing back, the teal clamped gently in his mud-brown jaws.

Back in the blind he sat quivering at my side, not from the cold but from eagerness for the next retrieve.

A pair of teal appeared to my left, ten o'clock low. I crouched behind the brush screen. They topped the trees, banked to port, then buzzed in fast and low. I rose, swung, and fired—two rapid shots . . .

Both birds fell within twenty feet of the blind. Easy retrieves for Jake.

By eleven o'clock the action has died. We see no more birds in the sky. Even the overeager shooters across the swamp have packed it in for the day. "Time for lunch, Jake," I say. "Let's go." We wade out to pick up the decoys.

The ice has melted on the duckboards, so going out is a lot easier than coming in. The only business left for us is to find that early wood duck I'd dropped. I have a rough line on it and we walk the edge of the timber, hunting it up. Jake spots it before I do—a drake with a magnificent comb. He picks it up and comes wagging back toward me, proud of his morning's work. As well he should be.

But Jake's day isn't finished yet. When we get to the blind of the guys who'd jumped the gun, Jake's head goes up and he stares into a field grown man-high with brittle, brown puckerbrush. His nostrils flare in and out as he sucks in fresh bird scent. Perhaps there's a duck in there that the other guys couldn't retrieve. "Fetch dead!"

Jake's eyes light up and he bulls his way into the thick stuff, hunting as he would for a nearby grouse or woodcock in the uplands, circling out on the wind, then working back toward me into it, his head held high for the scent. At a little teepee of weed he stops, sticks his head into the pile, and comes up with a plump, dead widgeon.

A perfect end to a perfect hunt.

Jake comes from Labrador show stock. He was bred for looks and temperament, not hunting ability. How then to account for his considerable talents in the field and more significantly the speed with which he learned to use them? Was his keenness to hunt already there when I got him, deeply immersed in his bloodlines and only waiting to be coaxed out, or was he motivated to hunt by contact and competition with his black Lab mentor, the inimitable Luke? As to tactics, Luke certainly taught Jake a lot—but only about upland game. Luke and I rarely hunted waterfowl, and never with Jake during his puppyhood, so how did the younger dog get duckwise so fast when we finally got around to hunting them?

During his eleventh year, Jake was diagnosed with diabetes. Our veterinarian, Jean Ceglowski, put him on a low-fat diet that reduced his weight from seventy-five pounds to sixty, and my wife and I had to give him insulin shots twice a day, morning and evening. He was still full of vim and vigor, as good as ever in the field, but after all, he was about to turn twelve years old. I decided it was time to start all over again, to start training a replacement Labrador with Jake's assistance, just as Luke had taught Jake the ropes during his puppyhood. It was a hard decision—an admission to myself that the best dog I'd ever owned would not last forever. This time I chose a black Labrador, not just to alternate the color scheme, but in hopes that the new dog would ultimately prove as great in the field as Luke had been.

Grace and Myron Morris in Zeeland, Michigan, who had produced Jake for me, fortunately had a newborn litter. I chose another male, whom I named Bart, as in Black Bart the California stagecoach robber. Due to the cataclysmic terrorist attacks of September 11, 2001, Bart's arrival was delayed. I was unable to drive to Michigan to pick him up, as I had with Jake. Air cargo had been temporarily disrupted as a result of the destruction of the World Trade Center and the Pentagon, so finally the Morrises decided to drive him to my home in Vermont,

door to door. Grace stayed home to tend the kennels and Myron undertook the odyssey. It took thirteen hours.

When Myron's diesel-fueled VW Beetle chugged into our driveway one afternoon at the end of September, Bart was nearly ten weeks old. The ideal time for a puppy to be weaned from the attentions of its mother and introduced to a new home is seven and a half weeks, no more than eight at the outside. Some nitpickers say the ideal time is precisely forty-nine days. At this magic moment, the pup is balanced on a very delicate cusp between obedience and independence. If caught at the right time, the puppy is primed to transfer the bonds of love and respect that it has with its mother to whomever next takes it in hand. Let that transfer be delayed too long, though, and the pup will develop a stubbornness of mind and behavior that's very difficult, if not impossible, to overcome. Whatever the case, the pup won't be near as "biddable" as it would have been at forty-nine days on the dot. Or so say the experts.

I quickly learned that Bart had a mind of his own, though it seemed at first to be possessed by the Imp of the Perverse. No sooner had he been released from his traveling crate on the afternoon of his arrival than he demonstrated the degree of that possession. When I called him over to me he came at a joyful gallop, stumbling over his outsized paws, tail flailing, coal-black eyes alight with glee, his capacious mouth bristling with needle-sharp milk teeth, and grinning from ear to ear. It was just as if he knew me, knew that I would be the firm but kindly master of his fate from that instant onward. Then he bit my hand.

"It's just a love bite," my wife explained, but still it drew blood. That was fine with Bart. He licked the blood off my hand, grinned up at me, and waited for more to well from the wounds.

Oh well, I thought as I wrapped a handkerchief around my mangled mitt, at least he's a peppy puppy.

Later that first day I took Bart out into the big field behind our house to let him run the cobwebs of travel from his infantile system. He followed dutifully at my

heels for about a hundred paces, as a bonding puppy should, but then sprinted ahead, nostrils flared and ears cocked, as if he were making game. Often there are woodcock to be found in the brushy edges of the field, and for an instant my heart leaped with joy. He's whiffed one—a God-given natural! Then he skidded to a halt, locking up into a perfect if puppyish point.

But it was not to be. What he'd pointed was a mound of fresh deer droppings, which must have looked to him like a cache of chocolate M&Ms. I removed him from the temptation as fast as I could. Lab puppies will eat nearly anything.

The next few days were spent in accustoming Bart to the sound of gunfire. I sure didn't need a gun-shy pup. At first I fired a cap gun while he was eating, so he would associate loud noises with his favorite activity. Then I had Louise bring him on a leash closer and closer to the spot in our back field where I was shooting clay pigeons—he couldn't wait to get there. He was ready for his first hunt. Next morning I took Jake, Roz, and Bart up to a productive covert of mine. It was already proving a bumper season for ruffed grouse. The previous winter had been mild, the spring dry, and there was food galore in the woods: loads of apples, barberry, thorn apples, beech mast, acorns. There were grouse everywhere, many of

them naive birds-of-the-year. The coverts fairly reeked with hot, fresh partridge scent, and the heavy dew of morning glistening from every sprig of puckerbrush only enhanced it. For any right-minded dog, I reckoned, this would be like walking into a pie factory just as the oven doors spring open. My theory has always been that a puppy can learn more from the example of older dogs than any man can teach it, and this would be the perfect morning to prove it. I'm sure Jake agreed. After all, he'd learned the skills of his upland craft from the master, old Luke. And Roz had learned the trade in turn from Jake.

Within moments of leaving the truck, Jake got birdy, back hair lifting, tail slashing, nose high at first to catch body scent, scanning the air, then low to the ground as he neared his quarry. As always in this critical situation, he walked as if on eggshells. As always he checked back to see if I was in position. As always I nodded to him, "Yes," and he stepped in for the flush. A grouse roared out from under his nose, I shot, and the bird tumbled in a spray of iridescent feathers.

"Fetch dead." Jake tore off for the retrieve. It felt good, as it always did—good day, good dog, good bird, and the great good relief when the teamwork plays out.

Bart had been standing beside me, watching all this with the air of a serious scholar. As Jake ran toward the fallen bird Bart's eyes lit up and he followed. He gets it! I thought. O joy! I'd witnessed this epiphany often before, and it's always a wonder—a new pup learning the meaning of the game from the deed itself. The excitement of the scent, the careful steps of the approach, the sound of the flush, the climactic burst of flurried wings punctuated by the blast of the shotgun, all fear or doubt forgotten in the stumbling fall of the game bird. On the instant, the pup learns the meaning of its life: The Climactic Retrieve, which this thrilling prelude has made possible.

But Bart had other game in mind. As Jake carefully sniffed out and mouthed the fallen grouse, the pup kept running his own course, paying no heed to nuance or ritual. He lurched and galumphed toward the nearest apple tree, where he smartly retrieved and devoured—a rotten Winesap, worms and all.

It was disappointing to say the least. Roz and Jake flushed half a dozen more birds that morning, grouse and woodcock, but Bart remained fixated on apples. On the drive home, as if to emphasize the point, he regurgitated them all over the floor of his Vari Kennel. The future did not look promising.

I've been a disciple of the late Richard Wolters ever since reading his book *Gun Dog* more than forty years ago. Wolters believed in starting a pup immediately on arrival in its new home, at the precise age of seven weeks (forty-nine days). He felt that allowing it to be on what he called "social security" (no training) for its first year was to waste the best training time of all—when a pup is most eager to please, and the lessons learned will be remembered for the dog's entire lifetime. Worse still, the longer you wait to start a puppy, the more likely he'll be to prove bull-headed when it comes to obeying commands. As to exposing Bart to gunfire at the tender age of ten weeks, Wolters said that gun-shyness in dogs is very rare, and that if you're feeding a pup the first few times it hears gunfire, it will associate the sound with a pleasurable experience. My older dogs had long since learned to

respond with glee to the mere sight of a gun, and even more to the joyful sound of gunfire. Bart instantly got the message.

Over the past forty years I've trained seven pups (five Labs, a German short-hair, and—most amazingly—a Jack Russell terrier) to be good, sound gundogs using the Dick Wolters method.

None have proved gun-shy, and all learned obedience and at least the basic hunting skills (quartering ahead of the gunner, checking back to make sure he's within range when they make game, keeping an eye on the bird in flight, and marking its fall when and if) during their first few weeks at home and in the field. My initial disappointment with Bart's behavior in the field was due to the fact that his immediate predecessors—the Labradors Luke and Jake, not to mention Roz (who was not a bird dog at all)—had all learned to find, flush, and (in the case of the Labs) retrieve birds by the time they were three months old. Because he got a late start, it took Bart a bit longer than the others, but by the middle of November he was doing the job he was born to do, and loving it.

I don't believe the Wolters method is the *only* method anyone should use in training a gundog, just that it's worked for me.

Obedience training and hard work with the retrieving dummy over the next week or two taught Bart the meaning of "Come" and "Sit/Stay," "Heel," "Fetch," and "Give." After the first few sessions, I was sure that he knew what those commands meant. Sometimes he actually obeyed them! On other occasions, though, he'd get that wild, devilish glint in his eye and the only thing that could lure him back to his senses was the offer of a dog biscuit. But bribery does not a sound gun-dog make. Was this just puppy playfulness, or did some deep-seated, ineradicable obstinacy lie behind it? Or even worse, was it a simple lack of interest where game birds were involved? Some dogs will never hunt.

LOUISE:

JACK RUSSELLS CAN LIVE TO EIGHTEEN, even twenty years old, and we told our children (or adult offspring as our daughter suggests) that she might very well outlive us and become part of our estate. They'd better decide who would inherit her. But, again, a strange tragedy struck, just as Bart arrived.

An e-mail from Bob to writer John Holt.

November 5, 2001: This is one of the saddest days of my life, Louise's too. We had to put Roz down this morning. She had pancreatic cancer which came on swiftly about a month ago, lost her appetite and a lot of weight, moved very fast into her liver. Last night she started shuddering and panting, her abdomen hot and distended. She couldn't even drink water. I gave her a Bufferin, then when that wore off, a piece from a codeine pill. Louise and I were up with her all night, took her to the vet at 8:00 a.m. It was time. She went peacefully in about two minutes. I will spread her ashes in her favorite woodcock cover and hang her collar and hunting bell in a tall, tall tree. Roz was only nine years old. Jack Russells normally live to fifteen and sometimes eighteen or twenty years old. It is vastly, horribly unfair. God, how we loved that little girl. I'll miss her forever.

The dog breed identification books describe Jack Russells as "merry," and Roz was certainly that. Despite Bob's and my lifelong love of large dogs, specifically Labs, Roz won our hearts as no dog ever had, or would. We spent that day in mourning, weeping, holding one another, cursing once again the (acknowledged)

unfairness of life, even the foolishness of becoming so attached to our dogs. The tragedy of her death lingers with me and I still dream about her. (As did Bob. In fact, I don't think he ever recovered from it completely.) Unfortunately, it colored our experiences with Bart, who had arrived at our house just as Roz was showing symptoms of the cancer that killed her within a month.

BOB:

I KNEW THAT BART OFFERED THE ONLY HOPE I had of dispelling the sadness, healing the hole in my heart. But I also feared that the tragedy of Roz's untimely passing would put an unfair burden on the puppy. How could I give him the full love and attention he required when I was feeling so depressed? What's more, I'd forgotten how much sweat and anxiety the training of a new gundog entails, even in the best of situations. At first I found myself calling him Black Bart the Wonder Dog as in, "I wonder if he'll ever learn . . ."

He was a piece of work all right, handsome, intelligent, and so black that he went invisible when Louise and I took him out for his final walk at night. We had to put a bell on his collar to locate him in the dark, then run him down and catch him. Bart was very fast and thought this an excellent game. Oh well, it was good exercise for all of us.

Bart was much more "at home" in the house than afield. He was quickly housebroken—quicker than any of my earlier pups—and just as quickly learned to share Jake's dog mattress, curling up at the older dog's feet when they both felt like a snooze. Roz, on the other hand, would not allow him up on the living room couch—that was her territory. So Bart staked out the red hassock in the living room for his own turf, hiding under it when he wanted to be alone. When he got too big for the hassock, he turned his portable kennel, which was in the kitchen,

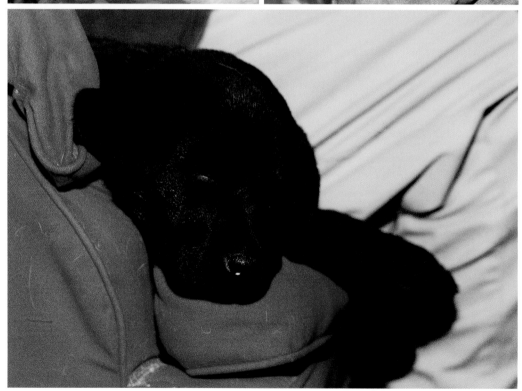

into what Louise called "his den of thieves." Here he brought everything he'd managed to filch from open closets, table tops, bathrooms, and the attached solar greenhouse where my wife kept her indoor gardening implements. In the thief's den we were likely to find socks, high-heeled shoes, garden trowels, bath towels, scrub brushes, Louise's Mephisto clogs, and once even a full bottle of Tylenol. Bart had a naturally soft mouth, so few of these items were destroyed, nor could he open the Tylenol bottle with its childproof cap and thus manage to poison himself. He had a thing for empty plastic bottles—Diet Coke, seltzer water, Sprite, or Fresca—it didn't matter to him what they once contained. He would squash them flat with his jaws—making a hell of a racket in the process—but only after carefully peeling off the labels and removing the bottle caps, holding the bottle with his paws, and gnawing on the cap, twisting and turning his head, until the cap unscrewed. He also likes it when we put a chunk of carrot in an empty bottle and replaced the bottle cap, a real incentive to remove the cap and destroy the bottle as quickly as possible. The only items he totaled, for some strange reason, were paper napkins, cardboard cartons, pinecones and sticks from the kindling box, and newspapers (preferably the *New York Times*, which we get by mail). He also swipes stuff from our neighbors, the Vickery's yard. Their big German shepherd Shadow hides his green tennis balls and his knotted rope chewies around their yard, and often after Shadow and his housemate Troika have been called into their house, Bart hangs around and searches out Shadow's treasures, as well as rotten potatoes that have been thrown out with the garbage and big chunks of wood. Then he scampers home with his loot. He is well named.

The good thing about all this benign thievery, the purpose of which was to relieve his teething pains (they last until a puppy is ten months old), was that if anything turned up missing in the household we knew at once where to look for it: his crate—his robber's roost—where he would lie on his belly with his forepaws draped over the hatch coaming as if posing for an illustration of the old WW II graffito "Kilroy Was Here." Louise says he's in his Kilroy mode.

Jake's old feline playmate, Spike, was still a member of our family and for a while, at least, he was the same size as Bart, so naturally the puppy tried to play "mouth tag" with Spike. In this game the animal that's "it" chases the other one until he can nip it. Then they change sides. But the grumpy, twelve-year-old cat had too much dignity in his old age and would have none of it. Where Spike used to play tag with Jake when they were both in their infancy, now he only hissed at Bart and threatened him with unsheathed claws. Bart diverted himself by mouth-wrestling with Jake, and the old dog still had enough puppy in him to play along with the newcomer. When Jake got tired of the game he had only to growl at Bart, and the pup took the hint. He would quickly find himself a paper napkin or the "Arts & Leisure" section of the *New York Times* and shred it into a good imitation of a blizzard. He was very efficient at shredding. In fact, he was so good that he would have made an outstanding Enron executive. A throwback to Buck.

Bart likes to wait until Jake is up on the couch, snoozing. Then he sneaks in and sits on the floor just six or eight inches away from the older dog's jaws and gives Jake "The Oogly Eye"—his eyes wide open with the whites showing at the top, his ears flattened back, an apprehensive look on his face (knowing he could get bit) but also a daring look, daring Jake to do something about this effrontery. Jake, without opening his eyes, wrinkles his snout and bares his fangs, uttering low, warning growls. Bart squirms his butt on the floor but otherwise doesn't budge. Finally Jake opens his eyes, raises his head, barks and snaps at Bart's face—purposely missing but hoping Bart will just go away and leave him alone. Bart usually does, until he feels like playing chicken again.

I'm sure that Spike likes to tease Bart, deliberately strolling in when Bart is calm and quiet, trolling his sinuating tail past the pup, and then Bart has no choice but to get up and follow Spike around, sniffing at the cat's butt. After a while Spike starts to growl, then spin around and bat at Bart's nose. But Bart is quick, like Ali with the rope-a-dope, shifting his nose to the side or back away from the cat's clawed paw.

Bart has learned the sound of a spoon scraping the bottom of a dessert bowl and will come from great distances to sit at my knee awaiting his chance to lick out the last smears of Jell-O or pudding or yogurt or ice cream. I know I shouldn't give it to him but I can't help myself. Then I go in the kitchen and scrub the bowl thoroughly with soap and scalding water.

LOUISE:

IN FACT, HE WOULD EAT ANYTHING, a characteristic of puppies everywhere. One late January afternoon during Bart's first winter, we let Jake into the meadow, with Bart scooting behind him. They suddenly disappeared into the tree line. I put on a jacket and took the whistle. After tooting and calling for several minutes, Jake finally reappeared and came toward the house, reluctantly it seemed. Bart didn't follow him as he usually did, but I could hear him shuffling around in the bushes. I put on my boots, called upstairs to Bob, who was working, and slogged up the meadow with some dog biscuits in my pocket. There he was, chewing a dead snow-shoe rabbit. I called him and blew the whistle. No response. I held out an inviting biscuit. Not the least bit interesting when he had a whole rabbit. Each time I neared him, he dragged the rabbit further away from me, so I just stood there and watched him eat it—fur, guts, bones, and all—while sneaking looks at me. Finally, he was finished and by this time Bob was outside. We snagged his collar and dragged him home, his stomach bulging like our boa's after a hearty mouse meal. We called Jean, who told us to fill a turkey baster with hydrogen peroxide, squirt it down his throat, and shove him outside. He'd vomit within fifteen minutes, which he did—the whole mess.

From the beginning Bart had a way of looking curiously at a problem with an expression on his face that seemed to say "let me figure this out." He'd cock his head to the side and stare seriously and thoughtfully. On a cloudy afternoon when he was about five months old, he was in the backyard, rolling on wind-fallen pine-cones. A clutch of squawking crows landed on the front lawn. Bart couldn't see them but he could hear them, his head erect and swiveling back and forth, staring at the sky, trying to place the sound. I was in the kitchen, which faces the backyard, and called him into the house. He ran in the door, zoomed through the house into the living room, which faces the front yard, and jumped on the sofa under the window, giving him a clear view of the crows. Tail wagging, he barked at them in his puppyish high voice with great enjoyment. He had figured out where the noise was coming from and where in the house he'd be able to see the crows.

Not long after that he was indulging in one of his favorite pastimes, chasing poor old Spike. They scampered under the kitchen table, then into the living room. To evade him, Spike ran under the sofa. Instead of trying to squeeze under the sofa after him, as other dogs have done, Bart jumped up on it and looked over the back, in time to see Spike dart out. He had figured out that Spike would exit from the back of the sofa, and he knew how to get a good look at him.

He still loves to snitch items—napkins, oven mitts, pieces of kindling—and bring them into his crate. One day last fall he grabbed a small log and, clamping his teeth around the middle, tried to get into the crate with it head on. Of course, the log was too long to fit through the door. He dropped it in front of the crate and stared at it for a few seconds with that thoughtful look, then hopped over it into the crate. Turning around and bending over, he grabbed the log, again in the center, and, tilting it, was able to work it through the opening of the crate at an angle. More recently, he tried to get a long stick into the crate crosswise, to no avail. He then backed up and turned the stick parallel to his body so that he could thrust the stick into the crate as though it were a sword. I think that's pretty smart.

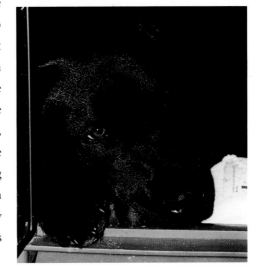

BOB:

BUT JAKE WAS BECOMING MORE AND MORE IMPORTANT TO BART. One dark April night when Bart was nine months old, I let Jake and Bart out at about 9:15 for their final pre-bedtime pee. They went ambling up into the field behind the house when suddenly old Jake went woof and took off into the dark like a six-month-old puppy. He sometimes does that when he whiffs a deer, and I shouted for him to come back, to no avail (he is getting quite deaf, especially when I order him to do something he'd rather not do, like stop chasing deer). Bart followed him at speed. I started up into the field and then heard a muffled whimper from Jake. Then another. Shit, I thought, the deer kicked him. I took off at a run. Then Bart came tearing back to me, ears back, eyes rolling—clearly upset. My eyes had by now adjusted to the dark and I saw Jake hobbling slowly downhill toward me. When he saw me coming he stopped. He was moving his jaws and I heard a faint clacking noise. As I approached him I saw what had happened: his face bristled with what looked like Captain Ahab's beard. He'd run afoul of a porcupine. I thought he'd gotten over that long ago, when he was nine months old and got a faceful of quills. It was awful. He'd gotten them in his left paws as well, both front and hind, and couldn't walk without causing himself great pain. He kept working his mouth to get rid of the spikes, but they only clattered obscenely and buried themselves deeper into his lips, tongue, and the roof of his mouth.

I ran back to the house, got the truck, and while Louise called the vet I drove Jake down into town. Bart looked on fearful, terribly disturbed, as I raced out of the driveway. Jake's face clattered all the way to the clinic, from time to time he groaned, but when he saw Jean Ceglowski, our wonderful longtime vet, waiting for us outside the clinic he immediately started wagging his tail, knowing that help was at hand.

She sedated Jake and we spent a grisly half hour with forceps removing quills from his snout, neck, chest, left shoulder, and both left-side paws. Some were even embedded deep in his palate. We must have removed a hundred quills in all. When I got back home, Louise said Bart had been standing by the door the entire time we'd been gone, whining and throwing plaintive, pleading looks in her direction. Jake was still unconscious when I carried him into the kitchen and lay him on his sleeping pad. Bart crept over to him and sniffed the blood on the old guy's muzzle, moaned softly, then gently licked it away.

Jake didn't wake up until midnight. All that time Bart fretted about him. I had Bart up in the bedroom with me and when I heard Jake awaken, we went downstairs and Bart saw that his big foster brother was alive, though still in some pain, limping as he made his way to the water bowl for a long, cold drink. By the next morning he was back to speed. Bart had been very considerate of Jake during his time of travail. It would be interesting to see if that attitude continued. The trauma of that spiking could have killed Jake, old as he is. That's what I worried about all that night.

On his first birthday, Bart learned how to pluck raspberries from the stalks after I showed him just once. I was picking and feeding Jake the newly ripened berries and offered some to Bart, but Jake bared his teeth and growled. So I called Bart over to the other side of me from Jake and pulled down a branch with some ripe berries on it, stuck one in his mouth, and he took it from there. Luke had learned this trick on his own when we took him on blueberry-picking expeditions in an overgrown meadow near a bird covert I hunted half a mile from home. Once he had discovered the joys of berry hunting, Luke also picked raspberries and blackberries in season at every opportunity. One hot August afternoon, my wife and I were harvesting thimbleberries in a huge patch across the road from our house with Luke chowing down alongside us. After about twenty minutes I noticed that the dog had disappeared. I heard rustling in the bushes at the far end

of the berry patch and figured it was Luke, but then—looking over my shoulder—I saw him disappearing rapidly downhill, headed for home with his tail between his legs. Uh-oh. . . . Clearly he wasn't responsible for the disturbance not ten yards from where we stood. I called over to Louise: "We'd better ease on out of here. There's something feeding on the far side of this patch, and it's neither canine nor human." With that, the creature reared up to full height and gazed, horrified, over the brush tops at us. It was an adult black bear. I don't know which of us was more frightened, but at that very instant of recognition, Br'er Bear swapped ends and took off uphill as quickly as Louise and I did in the opposite direction. Luke was waiting for us at the back door when we got home, looking shamefaced at having abandoned us. But I couldn't blame him. It was truly a scary encounter, but one that, in retrospect, merely added a welcome spice to life in these otherwise peaceful Vermont hills.

Bart was very good in public as well. Louise and I often took walks with the dogs along an abandoned railroad bed down in town, and when we met other hikers, even ones with dogs of their own, Bart was fearless and friendly. When I took him to the bookstore where Louise works part-time, he made lots of friends.

Women ooh-ed and aah-ed over him, just as they had over Jake when he was a pup, and Bart rewarded their affection with slurpy licks on the face. Even at his first visit to the vet, he was a very good boy, submitting to his booster inoculations without a whimper.

As a one-year old, he's a medium-sized Lab, about sixty-five pounds even though his father weighs ninety, and very muscular, a handsome dog, his black coat very shiny, reflecting the sky on sunny days—a sky blue tinge to it. I can almost see a distorted reflection of myself in his coat.

In the field, in the first few weeks, Bart showed some improvement. Instead of sticking to my heels he learned to follow his canine mentor, dogging Jake's every footstep, quartering with the older dog as he frisked the coverts for birds, raising his head to sniff the air whenever Jake did. He seemed much more nimble than Jake was at his age, scrambling over downed logs quite easily, only rarely getting high-centered on them. But unlike Jake at this age, or even Roz for that matter,

Bart had not yet flushed even a tight-lying woodcock on his own. In fact, he ran just inches past a few of the birds that Jake later turned back to flush. At Bart's age, according to my shooting diary of 1989, Jake had already put up half a dozen woodcock and four grouse by himself. What's more, Luke had actually allowed the pup to retrieve a few of them. At this rate, I was rapidly despairing of ever making a hunter out of my new dog. Then, out of the blue, came Bart's salvation.

Autumn 2001: One Sunday morning my friend and occasional gunning partner Jeff Piper called to invite me on a walk-up hunt with him and his good buddy Bill Iovene at Tinmouth.

"Bring Bart along," Jeff said. "He might learn a thing or two. Planted pheasants are easy."

It was a bright, crisp morning at the height of the fall color season. Jeff and Bill had left their German shorthair pointers in the Tinmouth kennel as we forged out into the first patch of pheasant cover: a long, wind-dried stand of field corn at the top of a ridge just south of the clubhouse. I walked the middle of the cornpiece, with Bill just ahead to my right and Jeff to the left. The plan was to call Bart back and forth between us as we proceeded through the corn, allowing the pup to cover the entire swath. Somewhere along the way he was bound to flush a longtail.

It went as planned, but at first not as well as I'd hoped. We weren't ten yards into the cornpiece when a hen pheasant got up right under Bart's feet. He looked nonplussed, watching her go. She flew straight ahead for a few loud wing beats, then curved to the right, rising against the hard blue sky well ahead of Bill Iovene. He deferred to my shot. I dropped her.

But Bart was still standing in place, grinning at the sky, Mr. Goofball. He gave no evidence of having seen or heard the pheasant fall. Then he sat down and busily scratched behind his ears.

We led Bart out to where the pheasant lay in the frost-glazed grass of the adjacent field. She was lying on her back, still kicking. Bart trotted up merrily—What

new wonders do you guys have in store for me?—then shied away in horror at the sight of the pheasant's beak and claws. He leaped back from the bird a clear three feet. I could see he was trembling.

Oh no, I thought. I've gotten myself a dog who's not afraid of guns—in fact he's gun blasé—but instead he's *bird* shy!

I felt like weeping.

"Not to worry," Jeff said, catching my disappointment. "She's bigger than he is, after all. She fell from the sky like a dragon, at least as he sees it. Let's just show him she's not a threat."

I held Bart, allowing him to sniff the pheasant deeply. His trembling eased. I put him down. Then Jeff took the dead pheasant by the neck and twitched her away from Bart through the thawing grass, as if the bird were fleeing. "Look, Bart!" he said in a high, puppy-wooing voice. "She's a-skeered of you! She's trying to get away! Get her, boy! Grab her, quick, before she takes off!"

Bart was doubtful at first, I could see it in his eyes, but after a few moments he steeled himself and pussyfooted after the bird. Jeff let him catch up to her, then let the bird lie on the ground, unmoving. Bart, still somewhat cautious, sniffed her

long and hard. He backed away a step or two, watching warily for any signs of life, then suddenly shed his puppyish fears. The rich, hot, primordial bird scent was too good to ignore. His eyes lit up, but with the shock of recognition this time, not fear. In that instant, I'm sure, he learned what he was born for: this was hunting. He pounced . . .

The next spring, on Memorial Day, we went to Tinmouth for a spring hunt. I killed another pheasant that morning, a big, bright cock, and Bart ran out to retrieve it as if the bird were the Holy Grail. Since that day he's been keen on any bird that runs, flies, or falls. Like Luke and Jake and Roz before him, he loves the game in all its rewarding fullness, be it grouse or woodcocks, pheasants or quail, ducks or doves.

All it took was patience. I should have known that from the start. You've got to take your time with puppies. But I'd been spoiled by the ease with which Luke and I had been able to train Jake to the nuances of the field. I now realize that Jake was a rare puppy, the quickest study I've ever known.

As with people, each dog has its own personality. No dogs of mine have been as keen for upland hunting as Luke and Roz, and none as quick to learn the game of hunting, as good at retrieving (especially waterfowl), or as gentle a companion as Jake. Bart may be tougher to teach, but he has other qualities that in the long run will define his style. Already he possesses a zest, an insouciance, an impish flair that sets him apart from his predecessors. He now knows the rudiments of the game. Once I've honed his rough edges, he'll be a splendid gundog and a boon companion as well. Can I ever love him as intensely as I have Luke and Jake and Roz? Of course, I do already now that he shares our love of game birds, and that love will only grow through time.

We can both look forward to a happy, game-filled future.

BUT THERE IS NO WAY TO PREDICT THE FUTURE, and two tragedies changed Bart's life and my life irrevocably. In November 2002, Jake's health suddenly worsened. During the past ten months he'd had several seizures—suddenly wobbling on his feet, then flopping onto the floor, foaming at the mouth, rolling helplessly back and forth—then just as suddenly he'd come out of it, shake himself off, and jump up, as steady as ever. Our vet, Jean Ceglowski, thought the seizures were connected with his diabetes. But by November the episodes were becoming more frequent, and the morning of the 13th, he had three in a row. We lifted him into the car and brought him to Jean. He couldn't walk into the animal hospital and Jean's staff carried him on a litter. "His heart is very weak, and so is his liver," she told us sadly after examining him. "We could try some things, but he won't last long."

Bob and I looked at one another. "Let's put him down now," Bob said, "before he gets any worse. This is no life for him." I nodded, as did Jean. He was sprawled on his stomach on the examining table, breathing faintly, his eyes closed. He opened them as we neared him and valiantly tried to wag his limp tail. We hugged him, and I kissed his head, then we both held him as Jean injected him. He died very quickly. The second dog in just over a year.

We had left Bart at home in his crate, and when we walked into the kitchen his black eyes shone through the gate. We let him out and he looked for Jake immediately. Then, sensing something was wrong, he jumped on Jake's cushion and sat quietly. It was another sad day, but not as difficult as a year before when Roz died. Her illness and death were sudden and unexpected; Jake had been sick for a long time and was already more than thirteen years old. He'd lived a productive and joyous life: the earthly equivalent of doggy heaven.

That same fall, while Jake was weakening, Bob was also sick. His stomach simply didn't feel right for much of September, and by October the doctor suspected gallstones. About two weeks after Jake died, Bob went into the hospital for a series of tests; he did indeed have gallstones, but the tests also showed a more insidious blockage in his small intestine. An operation revealed that he had cancer, emanating from the pancreas. He died quickly and quietly on December 18, of the same disease that had so quickly taken Roz. He used to joke about wanting to die before his most beloved dogs, Roz and Jake, and he almost fulfilled that ironic wish.

I returned from the hospital about 4 A.M. I'd left Bart in his crate, and he was jumping excitedly when I walked in the door but, sensing my mood, quieted immediately. I put a leash on him and took him out. The moon shone with a harsh blue light on the ice-covered snow. The world was very lonely and cold; a coyote howled up in the mountain behind the house, or perhaps it was Bob cursing at fate. Bart pricked his ears and looked up at me. We tramped into the meadow, then back to the house, and I lay, fully dressed, on the bed. Bart cuddled up. It was now the two of us, with Spike, the cat, ghostlike and remote.

For the months of November and December, Bart's life was topsy-turvy. With Jake suddenly disappeared, Bart spent many days alone in the house or, if it wasn't too cold out, snoozing in the car, while Bob and I were at the hospital. He stayed two scary nights at a kennel while Bob was operated on—a kennel where Roz and Jake had enjoyed many holidays, barking at other dogs nonstop or curled together in their own space. Here, poor Bart, alone and among strangers, was frightened and puzzled. He dashed joyously to me when I picked him up and tried to sit on my lap while we drove home. But even at home, it was confusing. Dogs like consistency and routine, and our lives those last two months of Bob's life were in turmoil. Bob would appear, too weak to play with Bart, then disappear into the

hospital for a few more days of tests. He had trouble sleeping and didn't want Bart in bed with him, so Bob slept in a spare room with the door closed. Every evening and again in the morning Bart would try to push the door open, unable to understand Bob's isolation. I tried to spend as much time as possible with Bob, but we both knew that Bart shouldn't—and couldn't—be left alone too long at one time. There were two routes to the hospital; the long way took more than an hour; the short way took forty-five minutes over a very steep hill, which was often icy. I was weary all of the time between the long drives, worrying about Bob and trying to keep some consistency in Bart's life.

The first few days after Bob's death Bart was subdued, I think, because he sensed my grief. Every time a visitor came, he looked up expectantly. When I said "Bob," he'd swivel his head, searching for him. I don't believe dogs have the brain or memory capacity to "miss" someone. They identify people by their odor, the sound of their voice, their body language, the regular routines they performed together. If Bob or Jake were to reappear, Bart would know them immediately. But I think he quickly "forgot" about Bob, and I became the touchstone in his life, and he in mine.

Because of our distress over Roz's death, we'd been lax about Bart's early training. Bart constantly jumped on Jake, especially his hind quarters, and we could tell Jake was in pain. No matter how quickly we pulled Bart off of Jake and scolded him, two minutes later there he'd be again, harassing the old dog. We finally resorted to buying an electronic shock collar, and Bart soon shaped up. We rarely used the bottom button, which gives a shock without a buzz. Rather, we used the first three buzzers, which make a loud sound right at the dog's neck and give a very small jolt. We were able to reinforce the desired behavior with Jake, and when Bart was out, we could keep track of where he was. I seldom use the collar now; he usually keeps very close and comes when called. If he doesn't, I only have to blow a whistle or show him a bit of dog biscuit, and he comes running and sits by me for his reward. I have a friend who scoffs when people talk about their dog's loyalty. "Just give me a handful of dog treats and he won't remember you in two days."

When Bart was almost seven months old I suggested that I take him to an obedience class; Bob agreed. He admitted he hadn't spent enough time with Bart. He was still mourning Roz and couldn't concentrate on the new puppy. I began the class at Petcetera, the pet store in Manchester Center, with trepidation. Bart was really a handful. In fact, the trainer called him Mr. Ants-in-the-Pants. I confess that we didn't do as much homework as we should have, but still the lessons refreshed Bart's earlier training. He relearned "Come," "Sit," "Give," "Heel," and he learned to walk on a leash. Although I joke that he graduated eighth in a class of five, the experience was good for both of us, and our bonding proved important by the end of the year.

My stepmother told me that after my father died she spent a lot of time with friends. "I could be out all day with other people, but eventually I had to go home to an empty house. That was the worst," she said. "It was so lonely."

I said, "I don't have an empty house, I have a dog." She thought I was kidding, but I wasn't. Cat people will disagree, but I have never been able to find in a cat the comfort and congeniality that I find in a dog. Even though Spike would occasionally purr and rub against me when I walked through the door, Bart was the official greeter, wagging his tail with gusto, running back and forth, sniffing my coat, jumping to lick my face. I'd grab him and hug him, and it seemed he was hugging me back. When I was busy he would watch me with interest or take a nap, but when I was depressed and morose he'd curl up next to me, often looking into my face with a mournful expression. I realized that it's so easy to anthropomorphize dog behavior because dogs are so quick to sense our moods from our body language and tone of voice. I didn't care. Here was a sweet companion, offering body warmth. I didn't feel as deserted as many people who have recently lost a partner.

There is another very important part to owning a dog, which kept me active every day. No matter how lonely and miserable I felt each morning when I woke up—or more likely, when Bart woke me —I knew I had to get up, put on some clothing, take him out, and feed him. By that time, I was wide awake, hungry for

breakfast, and ready to start the day. I rarely went back to bed—only if I hadn't been able to sleep during the night. Every evening before going to bed, I'd bundle up and we'd go out for a last trot in the meadow. His needs still shape my day and give it purpose. I'm not completely alone. The few times I've boarded him in a kennel and come home before having a chance to pick him up, the house has an eerie silence, a feeling of abandonment, even with phantom-like Spike there. When Bart's in the house, he fills the rooms with his excitement. He gives me a connection, he's a being I have to take care of and who needs me. Many medical and psychological studies have shown that single people, especially the elderly, are happier and less depressed if they have a pet; those with illnesses recover more quickly if they have a pet; the recently widowed, again especially older people, accept widowhood more quickly if they have a pet to help them make the adjustment.

Bart loves to be in the car, and he quickly became a good traveling companion, something he may have learned from Jake, who was a quiet and patient passenger. I have no problem leaving Bart in the parked car, for he will happily sit behind the steering wheel looking out the windshield or curl up on the seat for hours at a time. As long as the weather isn't too hot or too frigid, I take him with me to work

from time to time, letting him out for a walk on the leash every few hours; the rest of the time he sits in the car with a water bowl and a few chew toys, watching the action in the bookstore parking lot, his nose poking out the open windows. When Jake was less than five months old, Bob went to East Africa for six weeks. Although Luke was capable, and happy, to stay home all day, I didn't want to leave Jake unsupervised for so many hours. So five days each week for six weeks Jake spent most of the day in the car, in his crate. I would come outside several times each day to walk him, then he'd jump willingly back into the crate and curl up.

We all talk to our pets, from horses to goldfish. Dogs are especially attentive, making eye contact and seeming to understand and never disagreeing. They also learn very quickly to take cues from your words and actions; it's often quite amusing. Our dogs always became very excited when Bob put on his hunting boots. Although they hoped for an outdoor excursion whenever anyone in the house put on boots (or even shoes in the hot weather when I'm usually barefoot), the hunting boots were a cue they recognized at once. I remember Max and Simba running through the house, Simba barking, Max moaning. Luke would moan and throw himself against the door while Bob tied up his laces. Even sedate Jake would jump and run to the door, and Roz would bark nonstop. Bart leaps and barks when I put on my boots in winter or my walking shoes. It means I'm going out and there's always the hope he'll go along. But he's learned other cues, too. He watches me dress every morning, and if I put on earrings, the barking begins. I only wear earrings when I go to town. Dogs are so attentive to our every move that Bart can associate a simple act, such as opening my earring case, with a future result, going out—he hopes with him. Other cues are putting a stamp on an envelope (out to the mailbox), gathering the trash (out to the garbage barrels in the garage or, even more exciting, a trip to the town dump), grabbing my keys (a biggie—this means a ride in the car). He's learned to stay close to me when we hike in the woods or walk through the meadow, always keeping an eye on where I am; he's accepted the leash and becomes very excited when I pick it up, because he knows it means we're going out together.

I'm hardly unusual in my attitude toward Bart. The change in the human/dog connection is a rapidly growing phenomenon in America: Dogs used to be pets and working partners. Now many of them serve as emotional supports. In his excellent book on this subject, *The New Work of Dogs: Tending to Life, Love, and Family,* Jon Katz explores the societal changes that have brought about these new expectations we have from our dogs, and which they provide. As our society becomes more fragmented, with an increasing number of single households—whether by choice or because of jobs, divorce, separation, or death—people are seeking the reliability, devotion, and loyalty a dog provides as a substitute for human companionship. Bob and I were best friends as well as a married couple, and, with our children living three thousand miles away, we joked that our dogs were our surrogate children. But we also had one another. Now that I'm alone, I turn more and more to my dog for companionship. My children are still three thousand miles away. They have no intention of moving to Vermont, nor do I wish to move across the country. I have other loving family members and wonderful friends closer to me, but no one else lives in the house. Bart is my companion. The dog who was supposed to be Bob's hunting buddy is now my best friend.

Almost one year after Bart's last hunt with Bob, Jeff Piper invited us for a morning at the Tinmouth Preserve. I was anxious about how Bart would perform. Would he act up? Misbehave? Remember anything? It was a cold, bright November morning, the frost still clinging to the grass. I bundled up and attached a bell to Bart's collar. He hadn't worn a bell since the previous November, but as soon as I slipped the collar on him he began jumping excitedly—a good omen. He seemed very eager in the ride but sat calmly when I left him in the car at the clubhouse. As soon as we let him out, he began jumping, then circling the clubhouse, peeing on every bush, sniffing with his usual avidity. As we began hiking toward the pheasant cover, Jeff called Bart and he came immediately and began sniffing and quartering through the meadow.

Jeff led the way, with Jeff's wife, Kim, and I chatting several yards behind him.

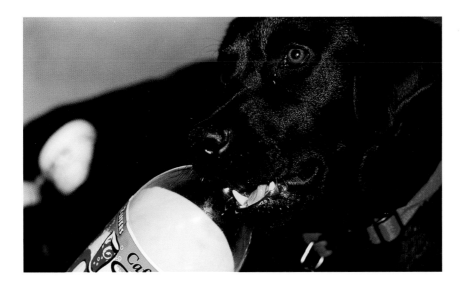

Bart would occasionally check to make sure where I was, but his nose led him. Suddenly Bart began getting "birdy" and a cock pheasant rose from a clump of tan grass, practically under his nose. Bart stopped and watched as Jeff raised his gun and squeezed the trigger. He excitedly followed the bird's trajectory, then ran to the fallen pheasant and started sniffing, licking the blood, and chewing on it. No retrieve. I was crestfallen. "Whenever I throw a stick or a Frisbee or the retrieving dummy he picks it up," I said to Jeff. "What's the matter with him?"

"This is a pretty big bird," Jeff said. "It would be like us picking up an animal four feet high. Don't worry. Let's see what he does." Jeff picked up the dead bird and tossed it. Bart again ran to it but wouldn't retrieve.

"Let's go on," Jeff said, stuffing the mangled pheasant into his game pocket. About ten minutes later Bart flushed a hen out of a rough cover near a spent cornfield. At that moment Kim and I were far behind Jeff and Bart, and Bart started looking for me. That's what I get for training him to stay close, I thought. Again, Bart followed the bird's descent and was excited, but he wouldn't retrieve it. Later, Jeff laid the birds on the ground and Bart came over, sniffed them, and started to pile dead oak leaves over them. Hiding his dinner?

We'd been out for more than an hour and Jeff suggested that we go back. "Let's end this on an upbeat note. Bart certainly has the instincts," he said. "He just needs reinforcement. He remembers a lot of what he learned last year, but he never really retrieved a pheasant, so we can't expect him to do it now. He's certainly interested."

We agreed that when Jeff has time he'll work with Bart. Meanwhile, I took two of the pheasant wings for training. Bob often trained the dogs by tying a wing on a long string, then tying that to a pole. He'd fling it out and reel it back in once the puppy had it in his mouth. I tried this with Bart, but he still wanted to munch rather than bring it to me.

Still, his instincts, excitement, and attention in the field that morning convinced me and Jeff that, had Bob lived and worked with him, Bart would have fulfilled his hopes for another fine bird dog.

Bob always said that the Lab is the ideal dog: highly intelligent, biddable, a great hunting partner in the field, and a lovable companion at home. Such an all-purpose dog can lead many lives, and it could be that Bart was fated to be a companion rather than a hunter. From the first day we had him he stayed close and wanted to cuddle, more so than any of our other Labs. We thought it was because he was confused about the long car trip and sudden separation from his mother and litter. But maybe that had nothing to do with it. When he curls up on the sofa with me as I read or watch television, always some part of his body—even the tip of a toe—touches me, but usually he's nestling at my feet or leaning against my legs. When I'm depressed he'll creep up into my lap and stare at me. Although I know that we dog lovers are unconscionable about attributing human behavior to our pets, when I'm unhappy it feels as though he knows and wants to comfort me. Perhaps that was his destiny from the start.

ROBERT F. JONES grew up in Wauwatosa, Wisconsin, a suburb of Milwaukee that at the time was still undeveloped. His outdoors play—fishing, hunting and wandering the woods with his friends—along with his avid reading of books by Edgar R. Burroughs, Charles Bernard Nordhoff and James Norman Hall, Ernest Hemingway, and others, influenced his life. As an adult, when he wasn't traveling in the wild places of the world, he wrote about them.

A high school All-American swimmer, Bob attended the University of Michigan on a full U.S. Navy scholarship, majoring in journalism and anthropology. He graduated with honors in 1956. He served in the Navy on active duty from 1956 to 1959 in the Western Pacific, including post-armistice Korea, Japan, Taiwan, South Vietnam, the Philippines, and many of the Pacific Islands.

A general assignment reporter on the *Milwaukee Sentinel* from 1959 to 1960, he won a Newspaper Guild "Page One" Award for on-the-scene coverage of a murder in 1960. He joined the staff of *Time* magazine in May 1960, served as a staff correspondent in the Washington, D.C., and Beverly Hills bureaus from 1960 to 1963, and then became an associate editor in New York City from 1963 to 1968. He wrote a then record twenty-two cover stories, mainly in the world and the nation sections, on subjects as various as the Vietnam War; urban riots; various coups, civil wars, and assassinations in Africa; Eastern Europe, India, and the counterculture.

Bob initiated the *Time* essay section as its first writer and traveled widely in sub-Saharan Africa and Eastern Europe. He joined the staff of *Sports Illustrated* in late 1968 as a senior writer until 1980, then as a special contributor from 1981 to 1992. He covered motor sports, professional football, hunting, fishing, and conservation, making five subsequent safaris in East Africa, the last in 1990 for *Audubon Magazine*. He traveled in and wrote widely on Latin America, the Rocky Mountain West, Alaska, northern Canada, the Caribbean, New Zealand, and Europe.

With both of their children grown, he and his wife moved from the New York City environs to southwestern Vermont in June 1979, where he wrote books and served as editor at large and columnist for *Shooting Sportsman* magazine and a contributor to *Sports Afield* and *Men's Journal*. His writing also appeared in nearly every outdoor magazine and in many newspapers and magazines, including *Audubon, Life, People, Harper's,* and *The New York Times*. He died on December 18, 2002.